THE HIGH SCHOOL GRADUATES OWNER'S MANUAL

THE HIGH SCHOOL GRADUATES OWNER'S MANUAL

A Practical Guide to Help You Get Your Adult Life Off to a Successful Start

Jim Egan

NEXT CENTURY
PUBLISHING

The High School Graduates Owner's Manual
A Practical Guide to Help You Get Your Adult Life Off to a Successful Start

Published by Next Century Publishing
Las Vegas, Nevada
www.NextCenturyPublishing.com

ISBN: 978-1-68102-177-5

Printed in the United States of America

DEDICATION

The High School Graduates Owner's Manual is dedicated to my teachers at Appleton West High School, and also to teachers everywhere, who invest their time, energy and emotions into helping young people go from a state of being naive, to one of becoming fully functional members of society through their adolescent years.

For most, your parents were your first teachers. This was both a necessity and a labor of love. Once you were old enough to attend your first school, your formal education began and was entrusted to professional teachers. Their primary objective was to provide the basics of the three R's, but more importantly, hopefully inspire you and teach you how to act and think for yourself.

Teaching is not an easy profession, and it gets harder every year. I am where I am today because of the efforts of my parents and several teachers that didn't let me quit when I might have wanted to, and always pushed me to do better than I thought I was capable of. Thank you for believing in me!

ACKNOWLEDGEMENTS

This work would not have been possible without the help and input of many people. As a first time author, you really don't know what you don't know, and if you are fortunate, the people around you help fill in the gaps. The encouragement I received was wide ranging, and it pushed me to treat this work seriously enough to make sure that it actually made it to the point where people like you would be able to read it one day.

Some of the contributions made to the work were small but extremely helpful, others were game changers. After my wife Joan read the 1st 6 chapters that were completed, she told me she thought it was pretty good; about nine seconds later she told me she thought it might be better if I added a quotation that was related to the topic at the start of each chapter, and some take away and actionable ideas at the end. Sure, that approach has been used in many other books, but it really made a difference in this one.

I think it made the work better, and in a way that went beyond the obvious. In going through the process of looking for just the right quote, for some chapters I read hundreds of quotes relevant to the topic I was about to address. It made a big difference in the content that wound up on the page. Thanks Hunz! You are the world to me!!!

My brother Dan Egan did the 1st edit of the work, and was a sounding board as to whether an idea or concept should be in or out. Dan's input was invaluable, and the fact that he took it very seriously was one of my first indicators that the concept might have an audience. Thanks Dan.

My mom's reaction when I told her that I had written a book was "I never thought you'd be the one to write a book". Despite that initial reaction, she bragged about the work to anyone she came in contact with, and will receive a nice commission for all the pre-sales she made for the work. Thanks Mambone! I love you. PEEB!

The following people all made contributions which improved the work, the marketing of the book, or just in general were helpful to me along the way. Many read it and asked me if they could forward it to their kids so they could read it. That was the best encouragement of all!

Thanks to George Moore, Mike Fenski, Jane Cook, Brian Krueger, Anne Glasner, F.P. Miner, Mike Muoio, Katie Glasner, Wayne Allen, Nikki Chaganos, Brandon Roth, Matt Frost, Marty Krueger, Charlie Wirth, John Harvey, Jessica Theresa Roth, Kerry Egan & Vince Hopkins. Vince asked me if he was in it when I told him I had written a book... Hey Vince, you are now!

And lastly, I'd like to thank the team at Next Century Publishing. Simon Presland, Tiffany Magner & Ken Dunn. Thanks for your patience and guidance. This would never have happened without your help and assistance.

Thanks and appreciation to all listed above, and anyone who made contributions after the work went to print. If I missed you this time around due to press deadlines, I'll catch you next time. PEEB!

CONTENTS

THE HIGH SCHOOL GRADUATES

OWNER'S MANUAL

INTRODUCTION

"Someone's sitting in the shade today because someone planted a tree a long time ago."
Warren Buffet

Congratulations! If you are reading this book, it's very likely that someone that loves or cares for you very much gave it to you. It's also very likely that you recently graduated from high school and are about to embark on the greatest journey of all time—life.

Your basic education is complete. For the last 12 years, that's what you did, with adults there every step of the way telling you what to do. That's about to change. Sure, there will still be adults all around you giving you direction, but what's different now is it's up to you whom you listen to and what guidance you will follow. In order to help you navigate this journey into the unknown, this Owner's Manual has been created for you. You own your future; hopefully, this Owner's Manual helps you make the most of it!

Forty years ago, I sat where you are today. For me, it was the summer of 1975. I was employed as a garbage man for the City of Appleton, WI, and was going to be starting at the University of Wisconsin at Madison in the fall. I was excited to be in that position, was looking forward to everything that lay ahead for me, and also had absolutely no clue in regard to what I would do, or how I would get it done.

Back then things were a lot different. There were no computers (at least no personal computers), no internet, no easy access to information. There was no shortage of advice, however. Everyone seemed to want to impart their wisdom to help me get my life off to the proper start. The problem was, I had no way to process or evaluate it. Some of the advice was spot on. If I had followed it, I would very likely be in a different place today, or at least gotten here a lot sooner.

Other advice I received was very well intentioned and sincere, but actually not so good as I look back at it now. I followed some of that bad advice, and paid the price. How would you know the difference, as it all comes from people that only want the best for you? The problem is, at a young age, you really have no way to tell the good from the bad, because you don't have life experiences yet to guide you.

The last 40 years for me have been a combination of highs and lows. I had huge successes, and epic failures along the way. I applied and followed some of the advice I was given, and also ignored much of it. One thing you discover along the way, is that when you look back at your previous life, you can see things more clearly. Often times you can see exactly what you should have done, as opposed to what you actually did. Wouldn't it be great to be able to know in advance the best path to follow?

Throughout this book you will find advice and life lessons that are time-tested and have proven effective. As I said earlier, much of this advice was shared with me; I just didn't follow it. As you read through the various sections of this book, you are going to come across things you may have already heard, read, or been told. Nothing I share with you is profound or original. However, everything I share with you will help you have a higher quality of life. You will be able to avoid some common mistakes that many young people make, and have insights and an understanding of how certain things work that most people don't master until a much more advanced age.

When originally conceptualizing this project, my thought was to target it toward college graduates, as that is the time generally assumed to be when young people cross the bridge to adulthood. However, as the various topics covered on the following pages evolved, it became obvious to me that this information couldn't wait until then. The reason is that decisions that you make in the next three months to four years can have a profound impact on how the rest of your life turns out.

I called this book *The High School Graduates Owner's Manual* because it provides guidance for elements of your life that you otherwise might never be aware of, yet if addressed early enough, could make all the difference in the world for you. It is often stated and generally assumed to be fact that at best we only use about 10% of our brains' power or capability. Probably even less with our computers. This Owner's Manual will help you tap into things that otherwise you might not have discovered until it was too late, or that you learned the hard way by making a costly mistake.

I wish you well as you set out on what should be a great lifetime journey. Be aware that the ideas and concepts shared with you on the following pages provide some basic things to help you get your adult life off to a smart start; the real magic will lie in the choices and discoveries you make along the way. You will have many challenges and obstacles to overcome as the years unfold, but the insights and guidance shared with you in your Owner's Manual should help you many times over along the way.

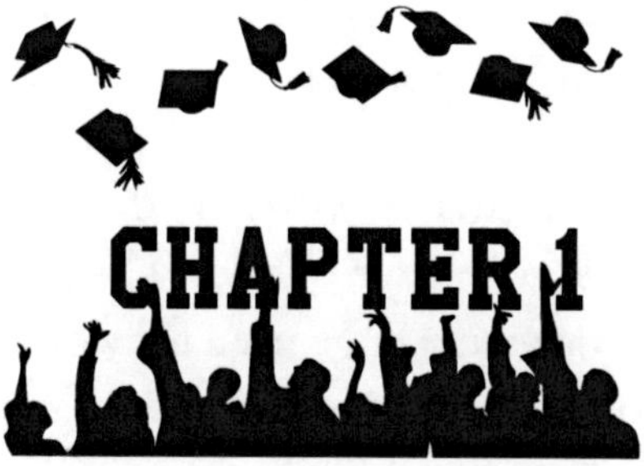

Investing. Start Now. Never Stop. Never Have to Work Again by Age 40/50/60... It Really Is Your Choice

"Invest in yourself.
Your career is the engine of your wealth."
Paul Clitheroe

Remember when you first started getting an allowance? Having money, even very small amounts of money, created demands that you make some choices. The easy choice was to figure out what to spend it on. The hard choice was to decide to not spend all of it, but rather to save some of that money to be spent at a later date.

Today that concept is more important than ever, as unless you pursue a career in healthcare, government or education, it is very unlikely you will receive any kind of pension when you retire. It is also very possible that Social Security will not exist when you reach retirement age. What does this mean for you? Basically, if you ever wish to be able to stop working, you will have to provide the funds you need to live on for yourself.

It wasn't always this way. When the economy of the US started to take off after World War II, the post war economic boom created a huge need for workers. Industries like construction, automotive and manufacturing created massive competition for skilled and unskilled workers. It was an era when if you landed a job with the right company, you would be set for life. You lost some freedoms along the way, but you could bank on the company taking care of you for the rest of your life after your working days were behind you.

A couple things have changed since then. For one, people started living a lot longer. In 1950, life expectancy in the USA was around 67 years old. Obviously the medical profession was not nearly as efficient as it is today, and people lived much less healthy lifestyles, with the consequences of tobacco and alcohol consumption not really understood at the time. The fact that people started living longer put huge pressure on the concept of a company paying you a pension for life. When this concept was developed, you would put your 40 years or so in at the factory or office, retire with full benefits and pension, and drop dead within five years. True example of a company man.

The life expectancy today in America is around 79 years old. We've added almost 13 years to our lifespans, (a lot more if you take care of yourself). The only problem is, you have to pay your way for the additional time you will be hanging around on the planet. Not a bad trade as long as you know what the rules are at the start of the game.

So you are really just beginning your financial life, and you have one thing going for you that will never get any better for you than it is today. Time. You will never have more time left on the planet than you do right this minute. Tomorrow at this time, you will have one day less left in your lifetime than you have right now. Don't think about this too much or you could get really depressed. Just be aware of it.

There's another concept to be aware of and understand. **The Rule of 72**. The Rule of 72 simply is a way to calculate the amount of time it will take the money you save or invest to double, based on what kind of return it is generating for you. For example, if your savings or investments were growing at a rate of 6 percent annually, if that growth rate remained constant, your money/investment would double in 12 years (72 divided by 6 (percent) = 12 years). If your investments were growing at a rate of 10 percent, your nest egg would double in a little over seven years.

Let's tie all this together. You are around 18 right now, give or take. In today's world of extended lifespans, you should have about 45-50 years ahead of you to do something before you will want to start living off your investments. At that point you would plan to live for another 25 years or so. In order to do so comfortably, you will need to have $1.5 to $2 million in retirement assets available. You can get by on less, and may wish to have more, but for purposes of this example, that's the ballpark we're playing in. How you gonna get there?

Now, I'm not a financial planner, nor do I play one on TV. For specific advice on how to get there, you will need to do your own research and likely seek out the advice of a financial professional. However, there are some basics I can share with you.

The stock market, over time, has returned an average of slightly over 10 percent a year. Historically, if you invested $1,000 in the stock market in 1900, and let it ride until the end of 1999, it would have been worth $19.8 million. And that with an annualized return of just 10.4 percent. Time is definitely on your side.

Understand that the stock market will rise and fall, based on events and cycles that you, nor almost anyone else has any control over. For example, the market experiences a correction almost every seven to eight years, meaning the value of the market will drop suddenly by an amount of anywhere from 10 to 40 percent, or more. When this happens, everybody panics, some people lose fortunes, and some people jump out of windows. For someone at your age, if and when this happens, it is nothing to panic or get excited about, as you have plenty of time to recover.

As you get older and your asset base grows, you will want to consider and likely invest in other, safer investments like annuities or CDs, where your money is protected against the wild swings that can and do occur in the stock market. With these tools you can protect your assets from the possibility of any loss, with the tradeoff being that you will not have the potential to experience large percentage gains during years when the market takes off.

CDs provide you a fixed return on investment tied to prevailing interest rates. When interest rates are very low as they are right now, they provide almost no growth but protect the money invested in them from any loss. Annuities are tied to the stock market, but limit the amount you can gain while protecting you from any downside loss. Most annuities cap their growth at 10 to 12 percent, which means if the market has a year where it sees 20 percent growth, your annuity will only return 10 to 12 percent. In the tough years when the market takes a dump and sees a 15 percent loss, your annuity will retain 100 percent of its value from the previous year.

As the years go by, your investment strategy should and will change, based on your asset accumulation and risk tolerance. You will figure this out, either on your own or with the help of an investment professional.

There is one thing you need to do today, or as soon as you start to receive compensation from any form of employment: start saving and investing. A good rule of thumb is to take 10 percent of each and every paycheck and stash it away. It's called paying yourself first. Many employers will provide matching funds to encourage their employees to do just that. While the range will vary from a low of around 2 percent up to a high of 10 percent or more, a 5 percent match is not uncommon. Whatever your employer contributes, make certain to have at least that amount withheld from your paycheck and invested in the company plan. By following this strategy, you instantly double your money, and over the course of your career will wind up with at least several hundred thousand dollars more in your pocket.

If you establish this pattern of saving and investing early, and make it a personal rule of operation for yourself, you will never have financial worries in life, and may be one of the lucky ones that is financially secure much earlier in life than the traditional retirement age.

Take-Away Idea: Time is on your side. As you invest over the years, keep the Rule of 72 in mind. The higher the rate of return, the faster you double your money.

Action to Take: Start saving 10 percent of any income you earn today. Make it a personal rule that you live by.

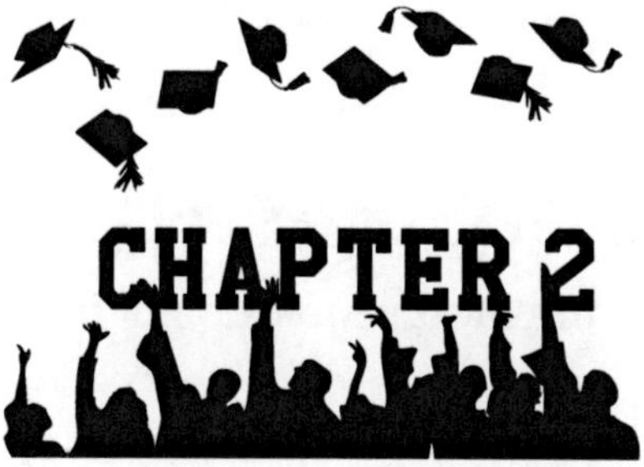

You Suck. So Does Everybody Else. It's OK.

"I am always doing that which I cannot do, in order that I may learn how to do it."
Pablo Picasso

OK. So maybe this isn't the nicest way to start a chapter, but I'm trying to make a point here. Many people, young and old, hold themselves back from trying something they like or might really enjoy because they think or feel that they aren't any good at it.

There's an overused statement that I've heard a thousand times over the years, and it is very true, but I never really understood what it meant. You've probably heard it also. In fact there are two versions of it:

1. Do what you love, and the money will follow.

And

2. Do what you love, and you'll never work a day in your life.

This is a good concept to fully understand, because it is basically true, and most people do not fully grasp it until it's too late.

At some point in your life, and very likely much sooner than later, you will have to get a job. And not the flipping burgers type of job, but a job that you will spend a good part of the rest of your life doing.

You've all seen the uber-successful people on TV being interviewed with everyone telling them how great they are. But if you talk to any of them and ask them how they got to where they are today, they will usually tell you it was through hard work, good teachers/mentors, and a lot of luck. Most of them initially sucked at what ultimately made them rich and famous.

A good place to look for examples of this is in the sporting world. You can make this analogy in any sport, but I'm going to use football because I grew up a Green Bay Packers fan when they were the best team in the world. The quarterback when I was growing up was Bart Starr. Bart Starr was a 17th round draft pick who barely made the team.

The record of the Packers during the first three years Bart Starr was the starting quarterback was 8 wins and 27 losses. Bart was not the starting quarterback for all of those games, but he started many of them. They were easily the worst team in football at the time, going 1 and 10 in 1958.

Fortunately for me, I was not really aware of them until the early 60s, when they were arguably the best football team of all time.

Bart Starr and Vince Lombardi's Green Bay Packers won five World Championships in seven years from 1961 – 1967, a feat that has never been matched or duplicated before or after in the NFL. Bart Starr is considered one of the greatest to have ever played the game. He won and was the MVP in Super Bowls I and II.

I relate the story of Bart Starr's journey through his NFL career because it has so many similarities to the process many successful people experience throughout their careers. When he was first hired, he sucked. Not his fault. In that era and at that position, everybody sucked when they came out of college. It usually took years to get enough experience and exposure to enough things that you would achieve a competence level that was acceptable. That hasn't changed in football or in real life.

Bart did not quit when things were tough. Instead he focused, worked hard, and did whatever he could to try and get better. It was not easy for him. Then the teacher, Vince Lombardi, showed up. There is an old cliché which you have probably heard, but is true in so many ways: *When the student is ready, the teacher will appear.* Bart Starr was in his fourth season when Vince Lombardi became the coach of the Green Bay Packers. All the struggles Bart had gone through during his first three years got him ready for the teacher.

If you aren't already familiar with these two men, go online and Google them. Their stories are inspirational, and their accomplishments, legendary.

Now back to you. It's likely there are things you are very interested in, have always been curious about, or possibly even have a passion for. That's what you should study, and that's the career path you should pursue. Here's why. With some exceptions, when you start out at anything, you are not going to be paid a lot of money. The reason is, you are not bringing any real value to the job. You might as well spend your 'broke' years doing something you enjoy.

Despite how often you were told how special you are while growing up, and no matter how many trophies and metals you were awarded for participating and/or simply showing up, real life doesn't work that way. From this point forward, they keep score. The only way to get ahead is to win, or to be great at something. The good news is, everyone can be great at something. The clue here is it's easier to be great at something you love or are interested in.

At the start of this chapter, I threw out the twin statements about doing what you love. I totally believe those statements are real, and here's the analogy to help explain what they really mean. As you begin a career and enter the real world, some of you will be more fortunate than others, will embark on a career that is easily monetized, and will have the means or the ability to end your work life at an early age, or retire early. Many people in this position choose to continue to work in some manner, because you have to do something with yourself, and if you've found the right calling, it's not really work.

For the majority of people at your age, you will work well into your 50s, 60s or beyond. I know that seems a really long ways away right now, but if you are fortunate, you will get there. Doesn't it make sense to spend the next 30 to 40 years doing something you love, rather than showing up somewhere for decades trading your hours for dollars? And as to the dollars, they start to get more plentiful as you become more valuable to your employer. The more value you bring to the table, the more money you will get paid. It makes sense that you will be more valuable doing something you love, rather than just showing up for a job.

This is worth giving some serious thought to. When I was your age, I had absolutely no clue what I wanted to do. I had many things I was interested in, but never sat down to seriously attempt to connect the dots to see where life might lead me. Things turned out fine for me because I was fortunate to have had great parents that instilled a sense in me that I could do anything, including make a bunch of mistakes. There were also many successes along the way, and those have a way of keeping you going.

Henry David Thoreau once said, "Most men lead lives of quiet desperation and go to the grave with the song still in them." Don't let that happen to you. Get out there and figure out what you were meant to do, and then go do it!

Take-Away Idea: Everyone starts out terrible at just about everything. Almost anyone can become great at almost anything. It takes focus, practice and time.

Action to Take: Spend some time thinking about what you are interested in, curious about or find yourself drawn to. Then start doing it, every day.

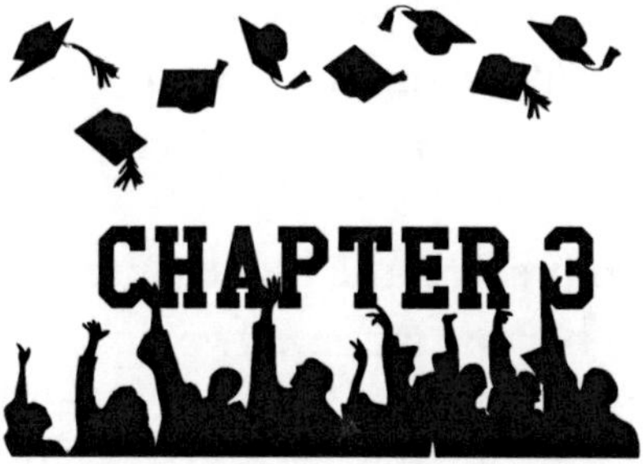

Give (Get) Yourself Some Credit

"Too many people spend money they haven't earned, to buy things they don't want, to impress people that they don't like."
Will Rogers

Right now, you likely have good or no credit. Many young people do not understand the importance of having a good/great credit score until it is too late. They've already screwed it up by the time they really need it and understand how it works.

Here's the deal about credit, and I put this near the start of the book because it is so important.

If you have good/great credit, you will pay less for almost everything as you go through life. If you have bad credit, you will pay more for almost everything as you go through life.

Your credit score is a three digit number that tells a bank, auto dealer, credit card company, retailer, mortgage company, etc., what kind of a risk you are to lend money to. Credit scores range from the 300s to 1,000. No one has a score of 1,000, and no one wants a score below 700 or so.

The lower your score, the higher interest rate you will pay anytime you borrow money, if you can get a loan at all. Purchasing a new or used car is a good example of how this works. The lower your credit score, the higher the interest rate, which means the higher the payment.

Let's say you have a job where you are making $30,000 a year. You want to get something reliable, so you are looking in the $10,000 range for a fairly late model used car with less than 50,000 miles on it. You've saved up enough money to put $2,500 down on it, so you're looking to borrow $7,500 to make the deal.

On the surface, this is a low risk loan for a bank, as you are borrowing less than the car is worth. If for any reason you stopped making payments, the bank would call the Repo man, and one morning when you planned to drive to work, you would come out of your apartment and your car would be gone. Easy Peasy.

But we know you will be making all your payments on time, so that will not be a problem. However, your monthly payment will be directly impacted by what your credit score was before you applied for this loan. If you have good credit (at your age you haven't put together enough of a track record to have great credit), your monthly payment will likely be in the low $200s. If you have bad credit, but not so bad that they won't make the loan (take a risk on you), your payment will likely be over $300. This means that over the course of a three year loan, you could be paying almost $4,000 more for the same car, just because you screwed up your credit score.

Here's something to be very aware of: it is very easy to attain and keep a good to great credit score; however, it is even easier to screw up your credit score and pay more for every major thing you purchase for the rest of your life.

For those of you going to a four year college away from home in the fall, one of the first things you will notice when you arrive on campus is the overly peppy young people dressed in very colorful clothes offering you a free T-Shirt or other gewgaw simply for filling out a credit card application. They assure you that you will be instantly approved, and it's very likely you will. You now have a piece of plastic in your pocket that can get you anything you want, any time you want it.

For some, that first week of college is the beginning of the end of their good credit score. They are excited to have the card, and they head straight to the mall, the Apple store or the bookstore, and try it out. They roll up a balance, and only pay the minimum payment required each month, or even worse, start to miss payments entirely because they ran out of money before they ran out of month. This begins a pattern that they will have a difficult time getting out of, if they ever do.

Here's the thing about racking up credit card debt, or debt of any kind. It means a good percentage of your future earnings must go to pay for something you did last week, last month, or even last year. Think about that. At your age, if you have a job, you will likely be working for a low or maybe even minimum wage. Although the credit limit on your new credit card will also be fairly low ($1,000 or less), how many hours will you have to work to pay off a debt of $700, $800, or $900? Accumulating debt at an early age can put you in a downward cycle that also means you start paying more for everything you buy from this point forward.

In addition, the rate of interest you will pay on any balances will vary widely. Most credit cards start out with an introductory rate that is relatively low. However, once the introductory period is over, the rates on any balances will increase, usually up to around 12 or 13 percent. With interest rates currently in the low single digits, that's not a good deal for you. Miss or be late on a payment or two, and that interest rate will shoot up to 29 percent or more.

Let's take the same scenario of the first week on campus, but with a much different outcome. Armed with the knowledge you have gained from this chapter, when you see the overly happy kids at the credit card table, you go up, get your free T-Shirt, fill out the app, and get your new piece of plastic like everybody else. But instead of going to the mall, the Apple store or the book store and make impulse purchases of things you want but don't need, you make a planned purchase for an item at a nominal cost. At the end of the billing cycle when the bill for your new credit card arrives, you pay it off in full. This way, you pay no interest, and begin to build a credit record that could save you hundreds of thousands of dollars over the course of your lifetime.

In addition, by taking this approach to building your credit score, the amount of credit available to you will increase rapidly. Early in your credit life you should just let it accumulate. There are times when it makes sense to purchase larger items on credit that cost much more, but always take the approach whenever possible to pay off your balance in full every month. The money you will save over your lifetime will be huge.

Make it a priority to burn this approach to managing your good credit into your brain. As stated earlier, it's very easy to have poor or great credit. It comes down to you having a plan in advance for dealing with credit. Set a standard of excellence for yourself in regard to how you will handle credit as it is made available to you.

Take-Away Idea: Your credit score impacts the cost of every major purchase you will make for the rest of your life. The higher your credit score, the less you will pay for anything you ever finance, such as cars, a home, etc.

Action to Take: If you don't have one already, apply for a major credit card. Make nominal purchases with it, and pay your balance off in full every month. If you already have a credit card, do whatever you can to pay your balance off in full every month. Always make all payments for any bills you have on time.

Where Do Great Ideas Come From?

"Think left and think right and think low and think high. Oh, the thinks you can think up if only you try!"
Dr. Suess

Great ideas are everywhere.

Think about this. When your grandparents were your age, computers and cell phones didn't exist. Then somebody had an idea. When your parents were your age, cell phones and computers had been invented, but they were primitive by today's standards. Then somebody had the idea to add apps and other tools. When your kids are your age, what might exist that does not exist today, but which everyone will have on their desk or in their pocket? Who is going to come up with the idea that turns into the next big thing that no one can live without?

Cell phones, computers, and even something as basic as the Selfie Stick all came from the same place; someone, somewhere had a great idea. While the complexity of a concept and the commercial viability of an idea will vary greatly, anything new that didn't exist previously starts with someone having an idea.

It's very likely you have had great ideas over the years. People are always looking for easier ways to do things, shave time off of a project, or make the results of an effort better and achieve results faster. Kids are usually very good at this. Steve Jobs and Bill Gates were barely out of high school when they started Apple Computers and Microsoft. No doubt the ideas that combined to form these incredible companies started to take shape when they were your age, or even younger.

Let's take a look at the Selfie Stick. We all know where that idea came from. After endless frustration shared by the masses, someone said, "There's got to be a better way to take a picture of me and the person I'm with." However, it didn't happen like you might think and was invented before cellphones had cameras in them.

Although there are references of attempts to use something like a Selfie Stick going all the way back to the earliest days of photography, the person officially credited with the invention was a Japanese man, Hiroshi Ueda, who was an employee of Minolta. The moment of inspiration occurred when he was on vacation with his wife in France in 1983.

As legend has it, he asked a child to snap a picture of him and his wife, but once he gave his camera to the little creep, the kid ran off with it. That incident and the frustration he felt led to his designing, drawing up, and submitting the concept to the U.S. Patent office, which issued the patent for the "Telescopic Extender Stick" in 1985. End of Story? Not quite.

Even though the design and intended use of the Telescopic Extender Stick was almost exactly like the Selfie Stick many know and love (or hate) today, and even though it was produced and promoted by Minolta, the product never caught on. Why? Most likely because the world wasn't ready for it yet. Back then, the concept of taking a self-portrait did not exist with the masses. Cameras were used to document special events, like vacations, birthdays, weddings and family gatherings. Although some people did take a lot of pictures (like my mom), most people did not walk around with a camera in their pocket at all times like EVERYONE does today.

But the story obviously doesn't end there.

Go back to Europe in the early 2000s. A Canadian inventor named Wayne Fromm was on vacation with his daughter in Italy, and had the same frustration of trying to find people he didn't know to take pictures of his daughter and himself in front of historic landmarks. When he got home, he went back to the drawing board. After several attempts, he came up with the modern Selfie Stick, which he originally named the Quick Pod.

His invention fared better commercially than Mr. Ueda's, mainly because cameras had gone viral. The internet was exploding as a way to share information, and retailers like QVC had come on the scene making it much easier to get a good idea to the masses. In fact, it became so popular that it was knocked off and sold by unscrupulous manufacturers all over the world, robbing Mr. Fromm of some of the proceeds that were rightly his.

The process of taking an idea from concept to commercial success is one that is both eye-opening and inspirational. You've no doubt had great ideas. What can you do to turn them into reality? *The High School Graduates Guide to the Coolest Inventions of the Last 100 Years* will be coming out in 2017 and will be filled with examples and stories of how people took a great idea and turned it into a marketable (and profitable) invention. The last chapter of this new book will address how to turn your great idea into a commercial product, and the steps you will need to take to protect it and bring it to market.

If you would like to receive the first five chapters for FREE when it is available, simply shoot an email to InventFREEtoME@HSGOM.com.

So where do great ideas come from? They come from everywhere, but you have to know how to be aware of them, as they rarely come gift wrapped with a bow on top. They usually grow out of something you saw, experienced, or possibly even misinterpreted. You also have to know how to get them to market, which I didn't know back in 1982 when I came up with an idea that has been in the SKYMALL Catalog for almost 20 years.

Back in 1982 I was living in Cedar Rapids, Iowa. One evening, we had a monsoon like rain that lasted for several hours. When I woke up in the morning, I noticed there seemed to be movement on the screen in front of my fireplace. Upon further examination, I realized to my horror that the entire screen of my fireplace was covered with zombie like horse flies. Big ones! None of them were flying, yet all of them were moving. There had to be several hundred of them. Somehow, the intensity of the rain had driven these flies from the chimney to inside the apartment, but for some reason, they seemed incapable of flight.

I grabbed a cup of coffee, and sat on my couch trying to figure out what to do. If I started swatting them, I would have dead flies and fly guts all over the place, and I figured some of them would get a clue and start flying away, or maybe figure out what was going on and come after me. Unacceptable. Then I remembered that the vacuum cleaner that my parents had given me had attachments! Moving very slowly, so as not to tip off the flies, I got it out, hooked up the extension hose, turned it on and started to vacuum the flies off of the screen. Every one of those little buggers was sucked up into the vacuum without a single one escaping. A problem was solved and a great idea was born.

To cut to the chase, the product that has appeared in SKYMALL magazine for the last 20 plus years, called the Best Bug Vacuum, was put there by somebody else. Despite all my efforts, I could not get it to market. I didn't have the knowledge, and I didn't have the means. I still have the original drawings, but someone else came up with the same concept and was able to make it commercially viable.

Good for them! Today Amazon.com has 12 different Bug Vacuums to choose from. Not good news if you are a bug!

Take-Away Idea: Great ideas are everywhere, can come from anywhere, and it's likely you have them on a regular basis. Learn to recognize when you may have come up with something new. Ideas take time to grow and develop.

Action to Take: When you think you have come up with something new, write it down. Actively look for new concepts, and give them time to grow.

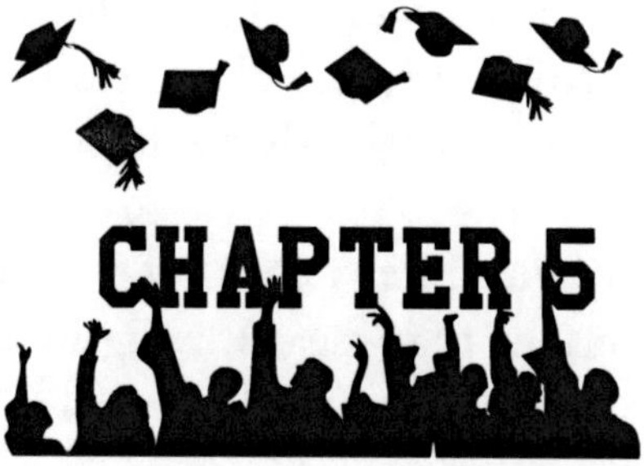

CHAPTER 5

Housing. How to Get Someone Else to Pay for Where You Live for the Rest of Your Life...Hint... It's Not Mom and Dad

"There's no place like home."
Dorothy

Really? No Way! Way!

This is one of the bits of advice that I was kind of aware of but never really grasped until it was too late for me to go this route. I wish I had figured it out when I was your age, because if you successfully execute this strategy, someone else will literally pay your housing expenses, and you could be financially independent much sooner, rather than later in life.

Earlier in this book we discussed the importance of having a great credit score, and also investing in yourself. This is one of the areas where that will pay off.

You have to live somewhere, right? And for almost everyone starting out that means living in an apartment where you have people you don't know living on the other side of your walls. You are paying rent to someone else you don't know, and take this to the bank, that is money you will never see again. Once you pay your monthly rent, that cash is gone.

Now let's assume you followed some of the earlier guidance provided in this book about investing in yourself and also making sure you have a great credit score. At this point, you have likely been working for a couple years and hopefully have a somewhat stable lifestyle. Your annual apartment lease is coming up, so what do you do?

Rather than renew your lease, it's time to go out and buy a duplex. This will require a down payment of usually at least 10 percent of the purchase price, so you will need to come up with at least $10,000 to $15,000 as you will likely be spending $100k to $150K on this, depending where you live. If you have been working for a couple years, you may have been able to save that up. Mom or Dad may also help you out on this one, but in the long run, you'll feel better if you do this on your own.

You could definitely find cheaper places initially, but remember, you will be living there also. You will live in one side and rent out the other. The nicer the duplex you can afford, the more rent you will be able to charge, and the better class of tenant you will be able to rent to. If you are very handy, you can consider a fixer-upper. However, if you are not, don't put yourself, or your future tenants, through this. You are the one that is going to get the call when something blows up in the middle of the night.

So now that you have moved in and found a tenant, you are on your way. If the math works out, and you got a decent interest rate on your loan, the rent you collect should cover about one-half of your monthly payment, including taxes. You now have your first passive income stream. Feels pretty good, huh?

A quick housekeeping note: do your housekeeping! If you live like a pig, so will your tenants. Keep the place presentable at all times, and live by standards that you hold your tenants to also. Keep the lawn cut and the snow shoveled. If you manage this investment properly, it will pay you back many times over.

What's next? Since approximately one-half of your living expenses are being paid for by someone else, it's time to start working on Duplex #2. Take most or all of the money you are saving on your living expenses, and save it toward putting together the down payment on Duplex #2. Along the way you will also be learning what it takes to be a property manager, building a strong relationship with your bank, and figuring out if this is an area you want to pursue.

By the time you have rented out both sides of your second duplex, your housing expenses are now being paid by your three tenants, and you are essentially living 'rent free.' But it's much more than that, as you are also building equity and creating assets for yourself that you will be able to leverage in the future. At some point, the mortgages on the duplexes will be paid off (with other people's money), and the rent you collect will be pure income, as there will be no payment due to offset it. Not too bad!

At this point, you have achieved the goal of living rent free. Someone else is paying for where you live for the rest of your life. Congratulations! Chances are you no longer live in the first duplex, and it's very possible you have expanded into multi-tenant properties. By now you understand the advantages and disadvantages of being a property manager, can decide how big you want to grow it, and how much time you wish to put into it. Hire good people you can trust to perform the ongoing maintenance, and you have a nice income stream that will provide for you long term.

Take-Away Idea: If you make you first home purchase a duplex, you will set up a passive income stream for yourself that could support you for the rest of your life.

Action to Take: Begin to plan for this now. Burn the concept into your brain so that when the time comes, you will be prepared and know what to do.

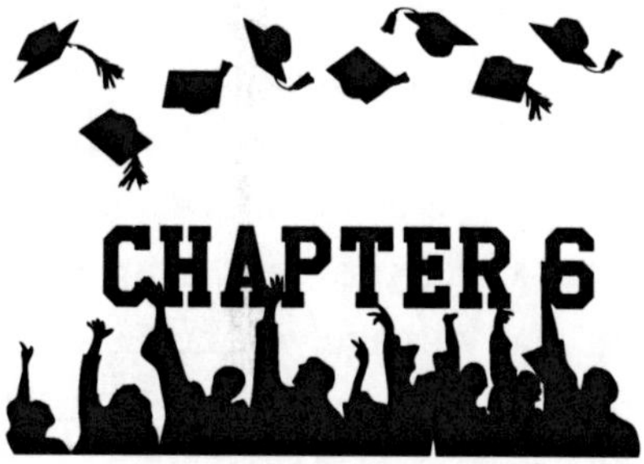

Don't Be Fat...It's a Choice...Be in Great Shape Always!!!

"If you are young and you drink a great deal it
will spoil your health, slow your mind,
and make you fat –
in other words, turn you into an adult."
P.J. O'Rourke

When I was a kid, we had a cat named Chumbley. Chumbley was a cat's cat, a drool machine, and could brighten up anyone's day. If there were stupid cat videos back in the day, he could have had a huge career. He was also not a small cat; in fact, you might say he was downright fat. He tipped the scales in the mid 20 pound range.

One time, I accompanied my mom to a vet appointment with Chumbley. After the initial pleasantries, the vet got down to business, and made a comment regarding Chumbleys' girth. I replied that Chumbley wasn't fat, just big boned. The vet looked at me like I was the dumbest kid on the planet and said no, Chumbley was not big boned, he was fat, and it was very unhealthy for him. Ouch!

You are at an age where you are or should be as healthy as you will ever be. Over the upcoming years as you age, one of the things that will age you faster and make almost everything more difficult is excess weight. It's a fact that some people struggle with their weight, while others seem to be able to eat and drink anything at all without ever gaining an ounce. However, as you age, your metabolism will slow down and keeping excess pounds off becomes more difficult, unless you form good health habits now regarding eating and exercise.

Let's break it down between eating and exercise. The easiest concept to remember is *Move More, Eat Less*. When I was your age, I was a distance runner. In high school, one of my friends' dads introduced us to a book called *The New Aerobics*. At the time, we were starting our junior year in high school and were bitching about how we hated gym class, specifically the block where we had to do square dancing with the girls. No activity has ever been given a more accurate name than square dancing. If you don't know what square dancing is, Google the term 'square dancing videos' and watch one for five minutes. You will understand exactly what I mean.

So anyway, my friend's dad suggested that we all read the book, make some notes, and then he would help us put a presentation together for the Phys. Ed department at school to do an aerobic program instead of gym class. It worked! We got out of going to gym class my junior and senior year of high school, while at the same time unknowingly began a fitness program that has kept me active (and fairly slim) to this day.

Here's all we had to do: run 1.5 miles three times a week in under 12 minutes. That's basically a not too far distance at not too fast a pace. Like anything else, we sucked at first, but we all took it very seriously because the reward was so great: no gym class! Over time, we got pretty good at it, as our per-mile times went down, and our overall distance covered went up. We found that we actually enjoyed it, and before too long were running on our own several times a week, whether it was part of our fitness obligation or not.

Having a physical activity that you do on a regular basis is a great habit to form now, if you haven't already. It will serve you well, and in many cases you may find you really enjoy it. In my case, one of the most incredible things I've ever done was a direct result of having been introduced to distance running as part of an aerobics regimen.

When I went to college, I kept up with my running, met some friends that were really in to it, and together we took it very seriously. I had an aunt who lived in New York City, so I set a goal to get in good enough shape that I could finish a marathon in a decent time. Specifically, the New York City Marathon. After a lot of miles run over the course of a couple years, race day came. A beautiful October day in New York City without a cloud in the sky. Ran the race in 3:08, and to this day, it is one of the greatest experiences I've ever had.

So that's how I moved more. Now what about eating less?

Let's go back to Chumbley. How did Chumbley get so fat? Simple. He ate everything he could get his paws on. He was fed a can of cat food every morning, and from that point on would spend most of his day mooching from anything the kids were eating. He had formed an over-eating habit and did not miss any opportunity to stuff his pie hole.

Overeating is a habit. I realize that some people have additional challenges in how their bodies are wired that makes it much more difficult for them to keep the weight off. Even for them, finding a way to eat less can only help their situation. For most overweight people, the core problem is they simply eat way more than they need to, almost all the time.

I like grabbing a quick lunch at Taco Bell on occasion. It's quick, fairly cheap, and tastes pretty good. If you ever go to a Taco Bell, after you order your meal, go sit in the corner and watch the amount of food some people walk away from the counter with as you consume your lunch. I'm not talking about kids your age either. You are entitled to put on a culinary display of mass consumption from time to time. I'm talking about the office workers that come in who are already 30 to 50 pounds overweight, and who stack their trays high with multiple items.

These people have made over eating a habit, and it is not good for them. For a good example of the amount of stress extra weight puts on your body, get a couple 10 pound weights and carry them around in your backpack along with all your other stuff for a day. You would definitely notice the difference. What about 30 or 40 extra pounds? You get the idea. The stress this puts on your joints, organs and furniture over time takes a toll. In addition, the extra weight makes your day to day activities more difficult.

Don't be like Chumbley. Make a conscious effort now to form good eating and activity habits. Identify what a good weight for you is, and find an activity you enjoy to help you get there. Having good health is a great gift to give yourself. Over the years, things can happen that will affect your health that you can't control. Control the things you can, and enjoy the benefits that come with it.

Take-Away Idea: Your actions and activities will determine your physical condition. Being overweight and out of shape will make your life much more difficult and less fun.

Action to Take: Find a physical activity you enjoy and make it part of your daily routine. Set a physical fitness goal for yourself, and make it a must-do. Be aware of what you put in your pie hole. Know when to put down the Chalupa.

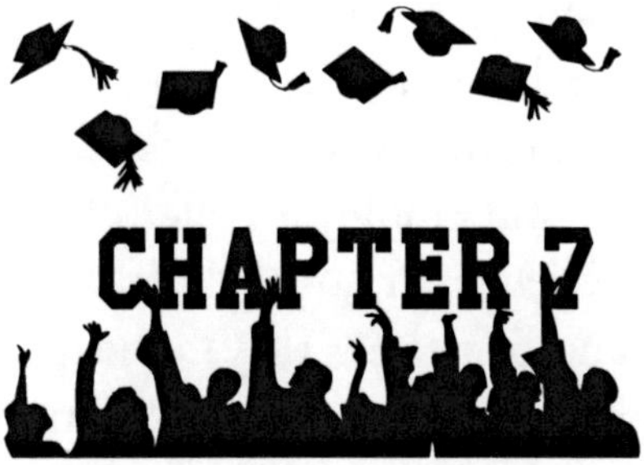

Your First Job. Get Experience at Working.

"Some of us will do our jobs well and some will not, but we will be judged by only one thing-the result."
Vince Lombardi

At some point, you will get your first full time job. Congratulations! The party's over…or maybe it's just beginning. A lot depends on what you do with it.

Many say that the first full-time job is when your education really begins, no matter how much schooling you have had. I would tend to agree. The first full-time job is really when you learn how to go to work every day, without the end of the summer, end of the semester, or other artificial signpost determining when it's time to quit and move on to something else. The first full time job has no natural end to it, and because you are new, minimal vacation, unless you go into education, which is a lot like going to school except you get paid for it with benefits.

You should approach your first full time job with an attitude of gratitude, and also one of an intent to learn as much as you can from your superiors. The attitude of gratitude because your employer is taking a chance on you. You have no experience, minimal skills, no track record of dependability, and somehow they hired you anyway. By the time you move on to your second full time job, all that will have changed. That is because of the chance your first employer took on you.

Your first employer can teach you a lot, like the importance of showing up on time every day and being ready to go to work. It's different here than at school, where sick days are expected, and not showing up at all (in college) has no real penalty or consequence, at least none that you experience in the short term. However, with what you pay to go to college these days, if you are cutting classes for any reason, you need to understand what each class is actually costing you. Your employer doesn't really show you how to show up on time and be ready to work every day, other than they will fire you if you don't.

You will also learn a lot by observing what goes on around you. The things you will see will be quite different depending on whether you are at a large or a small company. If you are at a small company, you will likely be fairly close to the managers or ownership, and will get to see how they make decisions, what kind of hours they keep, how they interact with employees at all levels, and whether or not you like the way the company is run.

If your first job is at a large company, your view of the work world will likely be limited to the department or discipline you are assigned to. You may be a worker bee in a hive of many others that all do a similar task to what you do, whether it's sales, production, fulfillment or some other activity that requires many people to perform it. No matter what the situation, it is extremely valuable to observe how people perform, and how they interact.

You may be familiar with *The Office*, the hit show from a few years ago, read the comic strip *Dilbert*, or watch any of the other TV dramas set in usually dysfunctional office environments. While these shows and comic books are meant to entertain, there is a germ of truth in the inspiration of those who created them. Many companies succeed in spite of the functionality of the people who work there.

You will notice people that are good workers to emulate, and others to avoid following the example they set by how they perform. Most managers have a pretty good idea who is giving it everything they have, and who is slacking off. When times get tough and the workforce needs to be reduced, the slackers are always the first to go.

The opportunity for you in your first job is to perform as well as you possibly can and only get noticed for positive things. You could be the funniest kid in the world, but at least until you have established yourself and brought some value to the position, it's a good idea to keep that side of your personality a little below the surface.

That being said, if you are lucky, you might find that you actually enjoy the work. As mentioned in another chapter, that is ultimately the goal of where ever you wind up working long term. It just isn't always available right out of the gate. If your first job is not in the field you want to be in, or you are not doing the type of work you want to do, you should use your first job to help you get your second job.

Even if you don't like it, plan to stay there at least one year if possible. This will help you establish a work history and get yourself comfortable with the routine of going to work every day. This will also give you the chance to think about what you really want to do and to start looking for a better opportunity while you are getting paid. It is much harder to get a new job if you have quit your previous position and are unemployed.

The first full time job is a great learning opportunity. Observe everything going on around you, spend more time with the hard workers than the slackers, and form your vision of what an ideal work life scenario is for you.

Take-Away Idea: Use your time wisely in your first job to observe, learn and think about where and how you wish to spend your work life. Understand that your first job is very likely a bridge to your next full time job.

Action to Take: Take the position seriously. Show up on time for work every day and make sure you create a good reference for yourself for the next position you apply for.

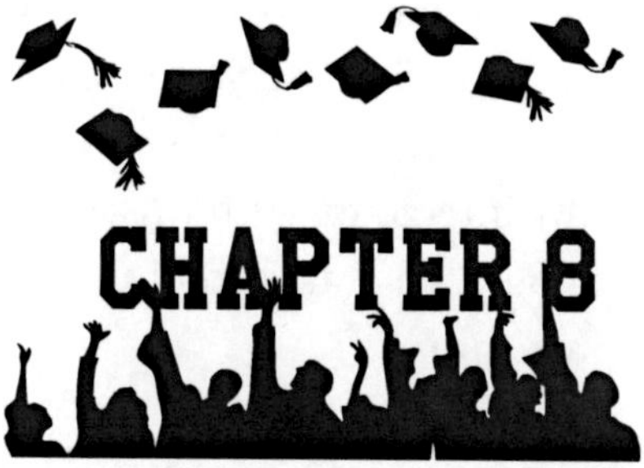

CHAPTER 8

Ink, Art and Self Mutilation

"Books are to me as homemade tattoos are to an inmate. Can't get enough of them."
Laurie Notaro

Are you positive that you really need that green thing on your arm (leg, back, neck, face…)?

A few years ago, my wife and I were at Summerfest in Milwaukee. We were in one of the tented areas, sitting at a picnic table taking a break from the sun. If you've never been to Summerfest, you should definitely experience it at some time. It's an eleven day music festival on the lakefront in Milwaukee where people from all over the world come to listen to music, drink beer, people watch, and interact with others. Sharing picnic tables with people you don't know or have never met before is very common.

While we were there one day, this young man came up and asked if he could join us. We said sure and made some small talk with him while we sat there. We moved on fairly quickly after he joined us, as we were planning to get up and go to see another band pretty soon any way. The young fellow we had briefly interacted with was unforgettable, and even though it has been several years since we encountered him, I'll never forget him.

How is it that I have a clear memory of someone I only met for a few minutes several years ago and never even knew his name? Because in a nutshell, he was a freak! He had a shaved head, with the skin on his head, face and neck tattooed to look like a snake. He had two knobs implanted under the skin of his head to look like little horns growing out of his skull. He also had his tongue split down the middle about an inch or so resembling that of a python. Just as when you see a two headed cat at the circus or freak show, the image was unforgettable.

There was something else unusual about the encounter. When the young man spoke to us, he sounded nice, talked normally, and except for the snakeskin head, horns growing out of his skull and snake slithering tongue, he was right as rain. That didn't matter. His appearance ensured that anyone other than an inner circle of family, friends and possibly other circus or carnival types would immediately pass judgment on this fellow the instant they saw him, and the reaction would not be positive.

Now before I go on about why you should not get a tattoo, or at least put some serious thought into it if you do, I want to say that I actually like tattoos when done professionally and tastefully, and think that many tattoo artists are very skilled. I have many friends that have tattoos, both men and women, and some of their ink is very well done and looks great on them. I also know many people that wish they never got the tattoos in the first place, and have gone to significant expense and effort in getting them removed.

As you begin the transition from childhood to the adult world, you will find that you will need help, kindness and support from others you don't know along the way. Those people would be other adults, possible boyfriends or girlfriends, and ultimately potential employers or spouses. At this time in your life, why intentionally do anything to send a message that would scare others, or at a minimum tell them directly that you are a person of questionable judgment who has already made one very bad decision that will have permanent consequences on your future?

The example I use is extreme but really not that unusual. There are hundreds of thousands of young people who have permanently hurt their chances of ever getting a shot at a decent job, spouse, or lifestyle because of a bad decision they made when they were in their late teens or early 20s. You are at an age when it is OK and normal to make mistakes; that's how you learn to not make the same mistakes again down the road. Very few mistakes will have such a damaging or permanent impact on your future.

Another thing to consider is 'what is your tattoo going to look like as you age?' Go to any outdoor event in the summer, and you will see people of all ages, shapes and sizes with green blobs on various parts of their bodies. This may come as a newsflash, but your body is likely going to change quite a bit over the next 20 to 50 years. While the tattooed image on your upper back may look sharp and crisp when it is created, 20 to 30 years from now it could look like Jabba the Hutt.

You are 18 right now. When you are 30, your mind will (or should) think very differently than it does today. Same when you get to be 40 or 50 or 60. There is not a single 30, 40 or 50 year old on this planet that would want or let their 18 year old self make a decision that they would have to live with forever. Yet that is exactly what you are doing when you get inked up at an early age. You are basically telling the older you to shove it.

Tattoos are not cheap. You are looking at a few hundred to several thousand dollars depending on whether you are looking at a nice butterfly on your arm, the classic tramp stamp, or full sleeve or legging treatment. And I don't have any way of knowing this, but I'm guessing getting tattooed is fairly addicting, as you almost never see a person with only one.

So I'm mostly done ranting and hope I have given you a few things to think about. I know that if you are not on the fence, but rather in the 'I don't care what you think, old man, I'm getting a tattoo camp' I likely haven't talked you out of it. There are a couple things, if you are going to go the tattoo route, you should consider.

1. Only have the work done at a reputable, established tattoo parlor that has been around a while, has a good track record, uses only sterilized equipment, and follows all requirements laid down by the health

department. If you can't afford to have it done properly, save your money up until you can. Don't cut corners.

2. Confine the location of your tattoos to locations of your body that will be covered up by business attire. Since most business dress codes these days call for business casual attire, you should keep your arms from the shoulders down ink free.

3. Do not have the face of anyone tattooed on your body. Usually this is done as a tribute to a loved one that has passed. No matter how skilled the artist is, it will invariably look like crap as your body changes.

4. NEVER, EVER, EVER have a tattoo installed on your face, neck or hands.

If you have become a successful author, artist or rock star where your lifetime cash flow needs are covered and you will never need to make a good first impression, do whatever you want. Until that is the case, definitely think it through before you take the cap off the ink jar.

In regard to piercings, gauges and other forms of self-mutilation art, in many cases, these do not have the permanent damaging impact of tattoos, as piercings can be removed, and the flesh and skin in the affected areas will mostly close back up and heal. Not 100 percent, but mostly.

Avoid gauges in your ear lobes, unless a career in the circus, carnival or other freak show is what you aspire to.

And if you work in the restaurant business at all, please avoid doing the septum piercing with the crescent barbell nose ringee… it's just gross.

Take-Away Idea: You are making a decision as an 18 year old that will affect you permanently and possibly impact the outcome of your life. How will you feel about this decision when **you** are 30, 40, 50 or 60?

Action to Take: Really think this one through before pulling the trigger. Consider putting it off for a while to see if the need to have this done remains so strong.

CHAPTER 9

Politics and the Media. Be Smart and Be Skeptical. Some Vital Information for the First Time Voter!

"Voting is a right best exercised by people who have taken time to learn about the issues."
Tony Snow

When I was a kid, the biggest insult my dad would use in describing someone would be to say they were a politician. To him, this meant that the individual was a person that didn't stand for anything, and would say or do whatever it took to get what they wanted.

Today, that sentiment is truer than ever. With some exceptions, the people that end up running for high office and winning are usually those that fit this definition to a T. The exceptions? Well, they almost never get very far in the process. So how did we get here?

In some ways, it's always been this way. You can go back to the days of Thomas Jefferson and Alexander Hamilton, or anyone one else whose picture you carry around in your pocket, and find statements to this effect. But it seems far worse than ever these days, and there is a reason for it: the media. Politics has become a blood sport, and the media, with its 24 hour a day news cycle is fueled by it.

Here's why this matters, or should matter to you. You have recently turned 18, and will be able to vote for the first time in November. If you do not make a focused effort to understand what is going on, you could be influenced by the media to cast your vote for someone or something that does not represent what is in your best interests. Many things are not what they appear to be on the surface, often times by design. For example, there is a hot button issue that you need to fully understand which will be on the ballot in November. It will directly impact you and your peer group. More on this a little later in this chapter.

Here is a quick breakdown of politics in the USA today. There are two major political parties in our country, Democrats and Republicans. There are also two major political philosophies, liberal and conservative. The vast majority of media are driven by a liberal philosophy, and by and large cover, support and evangelize for Democratic causes and candidates. If you wish to see and hear the conservative view point, you will need to watch Fox News or listen to Talk Radio. If you wish to be informed when you cast your ballot, you need to watch both liberal and conservative sources for information, and decide which side is more in line with your values. If you do that, you will be more informed and better qualified to cast a ballot than the vast majority of the adults in our country.

You hear all the time about how the nation is polarized on many issues, and that each side is totally set in their ways and locked into their opinion. But when you drill down a little deeper, you will frequently discover that the opinions people hold have been set in stone without ever giving two minutes of consideration to what the other side has to say.

For example, most liberals will state that they hate Fox News. However, when you ask them why or for specifics, they almost never have any, and usually will spout some left wing (Democratic) talking point about the Koch Brothers or Bill O'Reilly. On the other hand, most conservatives (Republicans) will watch only Fox News and listen to Talk Radio during the day, and never see what the other side has to say. Despite the opinions of most on the left regarding Bill O'Reilly, many conservatives do not like him either, because they say he supports the left on many issues, or does not come down hard enough on them like most conservatives would like him to. Bill O'Reilly would state that he is only trying to be fair and balanced. You need to decide for yourself. Don't let a parent, professor or boss tell you how to think and vote. Get educated about the issues, and cast an informed ballot.

At the start of this chapter, it was stated that if you don't pay attention to what is going on, you could vote for something that could negatively impact you and not be in your best interests. Here's an example that will likely be a hot button for one of the political parties next fall: The Living Wage.

The Living Wage is basically an initiative to raise the minimum wage to somewhere around $15 an hour, up from the current minimum wage of about one-half of that. Sounds pretty good, right? Get paid twice as much for doing the same work. Who wouldn't be for that? Well, very likely you, once you understand the potential consequences. Specifically that it will be much more difficult to get that first job, that summer job, etc. How will it impact your ability to get that second job that pays more, if you never got the experience from that first job?

Unlike what some in the media and many of the activists will tell you, all business owners are not rich. In fact, many small business owners barely get by. If the cost of labor to that small business owner doubles over night, he has only three choices: raise prices, reduce his work force, or go out of business. Many times, he will do all three, in the order given.

In some areas of the country, it's already happening. In Emery, California, they recently raised the minimum wage to $14.44 an hour. As a result, prices had to go up. Way up! At *LaneSplitter Pub & Pizza*, that meant the cost of a pizza went from $12 to $30. Sales plummeted at all three locations. The lunch segment of the business had to be shut down completely (eliminating hours and many jobs), and the owner, Vic Gumper, said it's very likely that after 18 years in business, he is going to have to close all three locations. These words are being written at least nine months before you will get the chance to read them. Google *LaneSplitter Pub & Pizza* and see how they are doing. Are they still in business?

The other problem with this scenario is the workforce itself. Due to the fact that the economy has never really come out of the recession that began in 2008, there are millions of able bodied people of working age not in the workforce right now. According to the Bureau of Labor Statistics as of this writing, over 93 million people from the age of 16 to 65 are not currently employed or looking for work. While this number includes many that no longer need to work, or have good reasons for not being in the workforce, the point is, there is a massive number of people that should be working, but currently are not.

If the minimum wage doubled to a 'Living Wage,' many of the people currently not looking for employment would get off the couch. A mature worker is much less risk to a business owner than a teenager or recent high school graduate. If the mom next door was willing to flip burgers for $15 an hour, she is going to get that job, not you. Every time. An old cliché states 'Be Careful What You Wish For.' This totally applies to the 'Living Wage.' A better cliché for today may be: 'Don't be careful what you wish for, be informed on what you vote for.'

Take-Away Idea: There are two sides to almost everything reported in the media today. Make the effort to understand where each of them is coming from, especially before you cast a ballot.

Action to Take: At least a couple times a week, watch the network news, and also Fox news. See how they cover the same stories. Be skeptical of what both sides say, and see which side makes the best case based on the facts, not opinion.

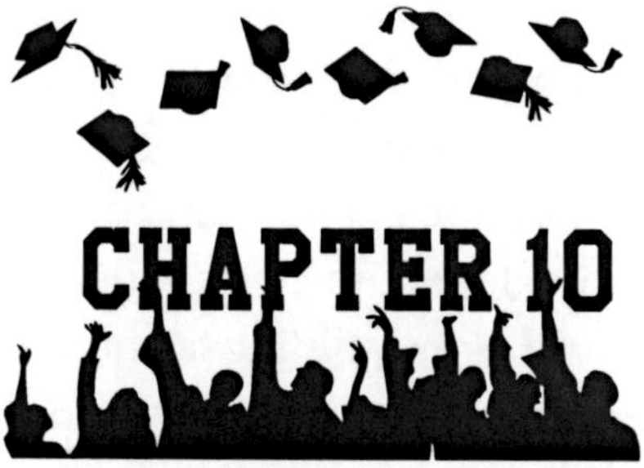

Go to College, Go to Work, or Work for a Year, Then College or Trade School

"You don't have to be a genius or a visionary or even a college graduate to be successful. You just need a framework and a dream."
Michael Dell

By the time you are reading this, you have likely already made this decision, but it's still worth reading as things may change for you over the next three to six to twelve months.

Many kids start their college prep in their sophomore or even freshman year of high school. The question to ponder is, will that be sufficient to have you properly prepared to make the right decision once your formal high school education is complete? Is going to college three months after you complete high school what is best for you? For many kids, waiting at least one year (a 'Gap' year) after graduation to decide to do anything is a much better choice.

Here's why. Today, many kids come out of college with staggering debt of $50,000, $100,000 or more. Debt that may take them a decade or more to get out from under. Being in debt for that long at the start of your working life will likely delay the development of your adult life, as you will not be able to begin building a household until you have it under control. If you are going into that debt for a degree in a field that you love, and which you know you will be able to get a good paying job upon graduation, then by all means, go to college if you can.

What if you have no idea what you want to do? If you don't know exactly what you want to do when you get out of college, are you sure you want to accumulate $10,000 to $25,000 a year in debt while you try and figure it out? And remember, you will need considerably more income than what is required to pay back your loans. You need to have enough income left over to support an adult lifestyle, which means car payments, insurance, food, rent or house payments, or basically a whole new set of expenses that up until this point, your parents covered for you.

In general, the majority of high school graduates don't know exactly what they want to go into. That's totally normal. It was the same when I was in your shoes. The difference is, 40 years ago, school was not expensive, and many kids could pay for it by having a part-time job during the school year, and working full time during the summer.

Today, college is extremely expensive. This is why it may make more sense to defer the expense and effort until you are a little more certain about where you wish to wind up. You are in the best position you will ever be in right now to spend some time figuring things out regarding your future. You have minimal obligations, do not have any kids or dependents (I hope you don't), and are in a position now where in some ways, you have more freedom than you will have at any other time in your life. If you use this time wisely, the next 40 to 50 years of your adult life could possibly turn out much better.

So let's look at the options. The first one is work for a year. There's a lot of upside to this, and understand, this is by design a temporary strategy. It will do a couple things for you. First off, you will get paid, which is good, because it means you won't be broke all the time. Being broke all the time really sucks. Getting a regular paycheck enables you to also begin to put in practice one of the strategies laid out elsewhere in this book, specifically, investing in yourself.

It also enables you to get through the process of adjusting to the work world and the concept of going to work every day. Even though this strategy is temporary, it is much closer to the real world that awaits you than previous summer jobs that you may have held that always came with an end date, the start of school in the fall. It's a great way to get a sense of what working full time requires, will expose you to things that are positive, and also things that are negative that you will want to avoid in the future.

The last thing working for a year does for you is gives you time to think about what you really want to do. If you use the year right, you will have the chance to look into possible careers, look into companies and corporate cultures that you may wish to be a part of one day, and get a better sense of who you are. It will also give you a chance to look at some things you may not have considered in the past. If you take this option, make sure you use the time off wisely. To simply work and get by with no focused effort to gain clarity is the equivalent of a wasted year.

One of the options you may not have considered is going to trade or vocational school after your one year break is complete. A friend of mine calls it "Skill School," and I think that name makes sense, as you go there essentially to learn a skill that can provide you with a very decent compensation for the rest of your life.

Here's something to think about. Many graduates of four year colleges come out of school with a ton of debt and realize they are not qualified to get the type of job that pays them the type of salary they need to survive. They soon figure out that they are going to have to go back to grad school for two or more years, take on a crap load of more debt, and then hopefully get a good paying job at some point down the road when they complete their advanced studies.

By contrast, Skill School is much cheaper than any traditional four year college, usually takes no more than two years, and graduates almost always have several options of where they can go to work when they get out. The reason for this is that Skill School teaches students how to do things that businesses are actually looking for and willing to pay top dollar for, many times in the manufacturing sector.

Recently I had a conversation with a recruiter for a manufacturing company in Appleton, WI. He made the observation that there is such a shortage of qualified welders, that for the foreseeable future, anyone that came out of a Skill School as a certified welder would have their choice of relatively high paying jobs anywhere in the country. I've never heard the same prognosis for journalism majors...

Although the unemployment rate in the United States is reported in the press to be a relatively low five to six percent, the real rate is closer to 15 – 20 percent. Yet skilled jobs go unfilled all over the country, all the time. There is an ongoing demand for Skill School graduates, so it is definitely worth looking into this during your Gap year to see if there are any fields you could see yourself thriving in.

The last option is to go to that four year traditional college after your Gap year. There is nothing like the experience of living on campus, participating in all the activities, going to the sporting events that go on year round, and just being part of something much bigger than you. Without a doubt, my time at UW was an experience that I value above almost all others. That being said, looking back now, I wish I had waited one year before I made the move to Madison.

It was my observation during my time at the UW that the kids that had taken a year off from school before coming to the university were much more focused, did better in class, and were less likely to fall prey to some of the many temptations of college life. Everybody is different, but over the years I have learned to lean to the option that provides the best chances for success. A Gap Year is a great option.

Take-Away Idea: Before going into debt to attend a four year college immediately after graduating from high school, consider taking one year off from school and spend the Gap Year working, and thinking about what you might want to do with the rest of your life.

Action to Take: Make a list of reasons why it makes more sense to go directly to college, and also all the reasons why it might make more sense to wait one year. Then discuss it with your parents.

CHAPTER 11

At Some Point You Will Have to Cut the Cord... How 'Bout Now?

"Growing up is losing some illusions,
in order to acquire others."
Virginia Woolf

When my father's life was near the end, my brother and I were with him one day, and one of us said that it may be time for us to grow up. We were both in our late 40s at the time. My dad looked at both of us and said with no fanfare or drama, "why start now?" It was perfect. The Baby Boomers were the first generation where many of the members have decided they are not going to ever grow up, and you can't make us.

That's what we like to think. The reality is, everyone gets old (if you are lucky), but not everyone turns into a codger. In an old Jefferson Airplane song, Grace Slick sang, "You're only pretty as you feel, you're only pretty as you feel inside." The same can be said or sung about aging. Despite what you may look like on the outside, only you determine when you mentally turn into an old fart.

So I think we can all agree that at some point you will mentally grow up. Here's the rub; in some areas of growing up, sooner is much better than later. Now that you have graduated from high school, it's time to begin to establish your own independence. Those two people that have been providing everything for you over the last 18 years have other stuff to do, and hopefully you can function without them.

Don't get me wrong. I was there when both of my kids were born and cut the umbilical cord for each of them. Many fathers have performed this ritual, and it is as beautiful as it is symbolic. There is another time when the cord needs to be cut, and that time is upon you. It does not have to be today or tomorrow, but you should have an independence day for yourself sometime in the next three to four years.

The best reason to do this is to consider what the alternative looks like. You may or may not be familiar with the term 'Helicopter Parents.' If you go to school in the fall, you will see it firsthand. There will be some kids whose parents will do everything for them, from moving them in, to setting up their room, to buying their groceries, etc. This is OK at first, because in many cases young people have never done this for themselves before. However, if it continues for the duration of the college years, there is something wrong. And the problem is owned more by the parents than the kid.

Taken to the extreme, the parent will continue to do for the child as they attempt to go into the workforce. From the human resource departments of most major companies, you will hear stories of kids that brought mom or dad to the job interview with them. Unless you as the kid have some ungodly skills that the company cannot live without, it's very likely that letting the parents come with you to a job interview will only provide the interviewer with some great water cooler stories, but not a future employment option for you.

Learning to function on your own is not that tough: it's just different and part of the maturation process. Your main job in this area is to help your parents let go. You do this by demonstrating to them that you are perfectly capable of functioning on your own. A good place to start cutting the cord is with your cell phone. I've heard stories of post-high school kids that still talk with their parents several times a day and also text them several more times to get answers and guidance about almost everything. What do they talk about?

Your parents care deeply about you and should want only the best for you, but they could have a hard time letting go. That's where you need to step up. Reduce your contacts with them. Set an informal schedule where you contact them on a regular basis, but get away from relying on them to step in and give you an opinion every time you don't have an answer to something. Google knows how to do almost everything. Go there, and get used to becoming reliant on yourself (with some G-help). The more self-reliant you can become, the more confidence you will have. This is another thing that falls in the category of great gifts to give yourself.

Your parents are a valuable resource and will usually help you in any way they can. They are a great sounding board as you mature and face many life decisions, as the experience base they have to draw on is much deeper than your own. Use them as a high level advisory source, but also seek other opinions as well. You are also in a time of your life when you are discovering who you are.

There's something really cool that will happen as you become more independent; your relationship with your parents will change from one of total dependence to one of respected friend and peer. You will begin to have different types of accomplishments than you did growing up, and different types of conversations with M and P. They will be tied to your professional performance, and at some point, be tied to your new family after you get married and have kids of your own. These are all great times in your life to look forward to, and you will have no bigger supporters than your parents. Their role will have changed, as will yours.

Here's something else to think about. At some point way down the road, you will likely become the parent to your parents. Huh? It's true. Once your parents get into their 80s and 90s, a total role reversal will occur, where they will need you to help them on a weekly or daily basis. They will depend on you to help them do things they can no longer do for themselves, both physically and mentally. At this point things have come full circle, and it will be time to re-attach the cord.

Take-Away Idea: You are entering a time in your life where you need to start to become independent, and rely less on your parents to do things for you. Know they will always be there for you, but understand it is better for you and them to create some space between you.

Action to Take: Have less daily contact with your mom and dad. They may have a hard time letting go, so be gentle, but firm with them in this process.

CHAPTER 12

Advice. How Do You Tell the Good From the Bad?

"I have found the best way to give advice to your children is to find out what they want and then advise them to do it."
Harry S. Truman

OK, this is an advice book. Here's a question for you. How do you know if anything you are reading is worth a crap?

Seems like a fair question. In fact, one of the most bizarre things about advice is that the more people care about you, the worse the advice they give you may be. Here's why: in many cases, the advice they are giving you likely made great sense when they were your age, but no longer is applicable. They may think the guidance they are giving you is in your best interests, because it's what worked well for them.

Here's my personal example of getting outdated advice from two guys that I loved and who really loved and cared about me; my dad and my uncle Jack. We were at my brother's college graduation in Minnesota. We were hanging out, having a couple beers, and they steered the conversation to how I was doing and asked if I was liking my first job out of college, which I had held for about 16 months.

My first job was installing and remodeling retail stores for Hallmark Cards. As I look back now, there was a lot about that job that gave me skills I have used ever since. However, at the time I was drawn to more creative endeavors, such as athletics, comedy, sports marketing, or possibly even writing books. The job I was doing was entry level, and although I was learning a lot about the work world and business, I was convinced I was capable of much more.

I conveyed this to them, and they both told me almost in unison that I was mixed up. They stated that a young person should be happy they had a job at a good solid company, and that one was not in a position to even consider making a change until he or she had worked there for at least seven years. I responded that I didn't like my job, and that there were a lot of opportunities in the Twin Cities that I might not have at the next place I was transferred to. I was advised that I would regret it big time if I made a change, and that I should continue to work hard, get promoted into sales, and see where things go.

I followed their advice, had four different positions over my ten year Hallmark career, lived in five different cities and became a top sales professional that won trips, rings and promotions. I moved on after ten years totally burned out, frustrated, and wanting to have nothing to do with any kind of retail sales ever again. So much so that I turned down an opportunity to take a ground floor position with a small retail start-up with 46 stores. The man I worked with at the time told me that they were going to be huge one day. That retail start-up has over 1,100 stores today, and the fellow I worked with became president and CEO. You may have heard of them... Kohl's Department Stores.

In another chapter we addressed how to approach your first job. My first job was actually awesome from a learning standpoint, as I was surrounded by great people, worked for a great company, Hallmark Cards, and have used the skills I picked up there for everything I have done professionally ever since. It was still not the best fit for me, and when I left, I was working 80 to 90 hours a week, was making very little money, and was at a point where working anywhere else seemed like the best option for me.

The other side of this coin is that someone you don't know as well may provide you with advice that, if you had followed it, might have changed the course of your life. Many of the concepts I'm sharing with you in this book were suggested to me during my early adulthood; I just wasn't smart enough at the time to act on the good advice I was given.

In one of the earlier chapters I discuss how to live rent free for the rest of your life. This advice was shared with me when I was in my early 20s by my wife's uncle. He didn't put it that way, or maybe I would have listened. However, he did suggest that I should make my first home purchase a duplex, save up the difference between what I was charging for rent and what I was paying, and apply it toward purchasing my next duplex at which point my basic living expenses would likely be covered.

He was right. I ignored him, and to this day I wish I had followed his advice. Without putting a pencil to it, I'm guessing that over the years I have paid out at least $500,000 in rent and payments to others just to have a place to live. That money could have been much better spent paying myself in the form of investments, which is essentially what you are doing when you purchase real estate and build assets.

The last thing about following good advice is that the benefits to you grow exponentially if you come across it when you are young and put it into action. Many of the concepts in this book will not have nearly as big a beneficial impact for a person if they are not discovered early in life. The older you get, the more set in your ways you become, and the circumstances in your life may make it impossible to put any of these strategies in play. The words you are reading are meant to give those who act on them at a young age a great advantage over those that don't discover them until much later in life.

Take-Away Idea: The earlier in life you receive good advice and take action on it, the better and longer it will serve you.

Action to Take: Find at least one suggestion from this book and put it to use at once.

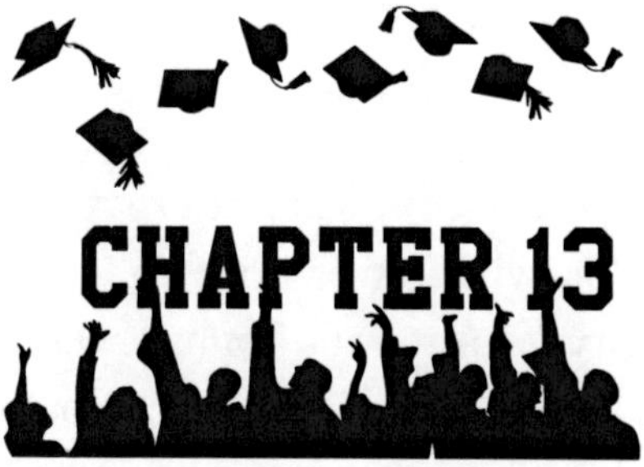

Does it Matter What People Think About You?

"You can't buy a good reputation;
you must earn it."
Harvey Mackay

Earlier in the book, we discussed your good credit and how it is easy to have either a good or a bad credit score. It came down to being aware of what it is, understanding how it works, and then making conscious decisions as you go through life to make sure you do it no harm. Oddly enough, your reputation works almost the same way. Almost, but not identical, as there is a significant difference.

Your credit score is very black or white. Either you paid your bills on time, or you didn't. There is very little grey area about this. All of your creditors periodically report your performance to the Credit Bureau. It doesn't matter if they like you or not. In a way, it's in their interest to like you, as a good credit score means at some point you may borrow money from them, and pay them interest (more money for them) if you don't pay the loan off in full.

Your reputation is your *Character* credit score, if you will. It is based on whether or not you are judged to be a person of integrity. Your reputation has been building since you were much younger, and it evolves as you move through life. You are still young enough that unless you are a really rotten kid, it is very likely you still have a good to great reputation. The unique thing about building a reputation is that so many things can contribute to it. You need to be aware that the things you do today could be having an impact on how you may be perceived by others later in life, when it really matters.

Think about the kids you knew in school that were bullies. What did you think about them? What did you do when you saw them walking toward you in the hallway? Would you ever invite them over to your house after school to hang out? Would you interact with them on social media? No, no, no and no. They have already ruined their reputation, and unlike when you ruin your appetite, a new one is not going to show up in about an hour.

Now think about kids that you know that have good reputations. They are the kids that do what they say they are going to do, show up when they say they are going to show up, and in general, are people you can count on. Once you've established a good reputation, like a good credit score, the important thing is to keep it that way. By now you know the difference between right and wrong. Doing the right thing is a good place to start, but sometimes things that seem right or harmless can hurt your reputation down the road in ways you don't think about at the time.

Social media is something to be very careful with, as in a way, you are creating a permanent record of your character and integrity by which others may judge you. The 'permanent record' that I grew up with was a paper file buried somewhere in the guidance counselor's or principal's office. Very few people would ever take the time to look at it, and unless you did something really bad or creepy, it's likely it stayed there until they cleaned out the files ten years or so after you graduated. Unsearchable, unavailable, and for the most part, not something that could come back to bite you.

Today, your online activities are out there for everyone to see, and create a digital permanent record that is easily reviewed if someone is so motivated. Anything you do online that is easily tied to you could have consequences. It could be some opinions that you post, or it could be something that you do that may have seemed funny at the time, and you wanted to share it with your friends. Young people have always done crazy, whacky things. And they may have taken pictures of what they did and shared those photos with their inner circle of goofy friends. Years ago, that would be where it ended. Today, once you put anything online, it's no longer yours, and you have no idea or control over how it is used.

In the business world, smart people know to never send off an angry letter or response to someone without having a cooling off period. I was taught if I was upset with someone and I felt the need to respond, to write the letter expressing exactly how I felt, print it out, and then place it in a drawer to reread and send out the next day if I still felt that way. I don't think any of those letters ever went out. If you ever have a doubt if you should or should not post something, take this approach. Wait 24 hours and see if you still feel you want to share it with the world.

So who might see it, three or four or six years from now? People that matter, like future employers that you might really want to work for. In an earlier chapter we discussed avoiding things as a young adult (getting a tattoo on your face for example) that you could regret in later years. This is the same concept. Today, almost all major employers do an internet search to gain insight into who you really are. Avoid putting anything online that you would not want your mom, dad, or your high school principal to see because these days, they probably will.

Another reason to do everything you can to protect your good reputation is that other people can try and negatively impact you, for whatever reason. This happens quite a bit in the business world. Today, there are many ways a customer can rate their experience with a business, whether it's Google Reviews, Angie's List, or simply putting a post on a Facebook page. 'Word of mouth' advertising can make or break a business, as people in general want to know what other people have experienced before they make a commitment or spend their money on a product or service they know little about. A company with a good or great reputation can overcome the occasional dissatisfied customer. If the reviews and posts show a pattern of poor service or unreliability, it's very likely that business won't be around very long.

Your personal reputation works the same way. You will have a word of mouth reputation from those who know you, and very likely an online reputation. Both are very important to protect and nurture. As you go out into the real world, your reputation will always precede you.

If you are a person of integrity and conduct yourself accordingly, you have nothing to worry about. If you are consciously aware of how your activities may impact how you are viewed by others, your reputation should be in good hands.

Take-Away Idea: Your reputation is something that enables people to make a decision about you before they get to know you, and is something you need to be aware of and protect, just like your credit score.

Action to Take: Be aware of how what you do today can affect what people think of you tomorrow. Be especially careful with anything you post on social media.

CHAPTER 14

Give Something Back

"Service to others is the rent you pay for your room here on Earth."
Muhammad Ali

If you were ever in the Scouts, you know what it is to be a volunteer and give your time to do something for others. When I was a Scout leader, I had the privilege of working with young boys to help them learn various life skills through the Cub Scouts and Boy Scouts. One of the things every scout learned at an early age was the importance of doing things to make your community a better place. Sure, we were big on hiking, camping, earning merit badges and helping little old ladies cross the street, but our stock in trade was being available to do things in the community that no one else was there to do.

Volunteering is about serving others, and it's another arrow to have in your quiver of life's foundation blocks. Even though sometimes it seems as if it's all about you, it's actually not. It's all about what you do, and consciously finding a way to help others is a great way to bring balance into your purposed life. People who have made volunteering a cornerstone of their life consistently say that no matter how much they give of their time and or resources, what they get in return is always much greater.

Your contributions to others will and should change over time as your life develops and evolves. At this stage, the one asset you have the most of to share is your time. There are good organizations everywhere that are looking for people that can lend a hand, whether it's a food pantry, animal shelter, or the local Senior Center. Just as in an earlier chapter the topic was finding something you love to do, the same approach can apply here. If you love animals, find an animal shelter or rescue center, and give them a few hours of your time every week. If you like the idea of building things, get active in the local Habitat for Humanity Chapter and learn what it feels like to help someone get their very own home for the first time. If you enjoyed hanging out with your grandparents when you were growing up, go to a senior home and tell the person at the front desk that you would like to go visit with someone that needs a friend. The opportunities to volunteer are everywhere!

Something else happens when you help others in this manner. You get a sense of satisfaction that your actions are making a difference. When I took over as a Cub Scout Leader for Pack 6, the Pack had seen better days. With the help and commitment of several other parents, we decided we would change things. Pack meetings were turned from 90 minutes of boredom, begging and drudgery once a month into a monthly event that rocked for the boys and their parents. Each month had a different theme that involved activities, entertainment, and excitement.

How did it happen? We got together and identified the core issue: the Pack was broke. We needed to figure out a way to generate enough revenue to fund an entire year of scouting activities without turning our Pack into a hoard of tiny sales people and/or beggars. Because many of the parents had some experience or connections in the foodservice industry, we decided to put our collective experience to work. We took over the back-to-school picnic at the start of the year, and ran a high-quality foodservice operation for one three-hour picnic. We served things like salmon, pork chops and chicken breast sandwiches in addition to the standard fare of brats, burgers and hotdogs. The picnic was a *huge* hit, and the revenue generated staked our Pack for the upcoming year. The boys still participated in the annual popcorn sale, but all other forms of fundraising were no longer needed.

So what if you don't have a lot of time or money? What about random acts of kindness? They say Karma never forgets, and if you make a conscious effort to brighten the day of someone else, that counts for something. It's not a substitution for contributing or giving back, but can function as a place holder until you have the time or resources to give back consistently and significantly. A couple examples of random acts of kindness that can make a difference in the life of someone include:

- Check "yes" on your driver's license when asked if you wish to become an organ donor — and tell your family.

- Pretend you are in the scouts again. Go on a hike and pick up trash along the way.

- If you have an elderly neighbor, offer to cut their grass or shovel their snow.

- If you know a shut-in, offer to go grocery shopping for them.

- Send your mom flowers, sometime other than Mother's Day, Valentine's Day or her birthday, just for the heck of it.

- If you received more than one copy of this book, give the extra(s) to friends you care about that will benefit from the information you have just read.

Over time, your ability to contribute may change. You may get to the point where you have more money than time to give, so your giving may shift from time to dollars. That also can be extremely rewarding because at that point, you can have a positive impact on a much wider range of people. It's actually fun to visualize what you could do for others if you had the resources. I do it all the time, as it's one of the things that drives me. One of my college fraternity brothers has buildings named after him on the

University of Wisconsin campus at Madison because of the huge financial contributions he has made. Imagine how great that must feel!

No matter what level of contribution you can make, whether it is measured in hours or dollars, make it, and make giving back a part of who you are. Through the accident of birth, those of us in the USA were born into the land of opportunity, with a lifestyle and freedom that are the envy of the world. Never take that for granted. Along the way, look for ways you can serve and assist those less fortunate than you. No matter how much you give, you will always receive more in return.

Take-Away Idea: You have been given a lot. You were born in the right place at the right time. Appreciate what you have, and look for ways to give back to others. Learn and understand the benefits of Giver's Gain.

Action to Take: Make a personal commitment to give something back, and then do it. Just as you will be setting up your personal savings plan, set up your personal giving back plan with the same level of focus and commitment.

CONCLUSION

"What's money? A man is a success if he gets up in the morning and goes to bed at night and in between does what he wants to do."

Bob Dylan

Thanks for taking the time to read the *High School Graduates Owner's Manual.* Hopefully you found at least one concept here that you have committed to making a part of your life from this point forward. Possibly several of the concepts on the previous pages made sense, and the more that you actually put in play and take advantage of, the more successful you will be, and the faster it will happen for you.

Over the next 30 to 40 to 50 years, I hope you will experience many wonderful things. Success, however you define it, is the one element that should be your goal in all that you do. If you have a plan when you start, the chances grow exponentially that you will realize your ultimate goals, and realize that success much sooner, rather than later.

When you get to this point in most books, you are at the end. However, with this book, you are at the beginning. There's so much for you to learn as you go forward. Hopefully you will continue your education, whether you do it right away, or whether you take advantage of a Gap year to better plan your journey. And once your formal education is complete, your real education can begin.

Jim Rohm once said, "Formal education will make you a living; self-education will make you a fortune!" Stay curious, and always seek to become more knowledgeable. If you don't know who Jim Rohm is, Google him and read some of his writings. He's big on self-responsibility and continuous improvement. His writings provide simple, common sense guidance that all people, and especially young people, could greatly benefit from, no matter what age you are at when you discover him.

As this chapter is completed for me, the next one is beginning, and I would like to ask for your help. The intent of the *High School Graduates Owner's Manual* was to begin a dialog with people crossing the bridge from adolescence to early adulthood. I included topics in this first edition that for me were easy outs, meaning things that were so obvious that the advice given would surely help anyone that made any effort to put it in play. Some of it may not be easy to follow at first (saving some of your paycheck instead of spending it all), but if a personal commitment is made and the plan is executed, the positive results are certain.

So what did I miss? What topic was not included that should have been included? What did you like best? What are you going to try and make part of your life plan going forward? I realize that for many, the ideas shared here will be put on the shelf for use and implementation at some future date. That's the idea. You have a life to live, and the concepts shared here will hopefully be like the programs that run in the background on your computer; they are there for you when you need them.

There were also topics like parenting, family dynamics and Sex & Drugs & Rock & Roll that were considered but not included in this edition. What are the things that you would like to see additional information on? Along those lines, there will be expanded editions coming out in the *High School Graduate* series that will go into more depth on certain topics, the first being *The High School Graduates Guide to the Coolest Inventions of the Last 100 Years* "coming out in 2017 (see Chapter 4 for info on how to get the first five chapters for *free*). What else would you like to know more about?

And I'd also like to hear what your parents think. What topics do they feel should be included in future editions of *The High School Graduates Owner's Manual?* How about any high school teachers out there? This work is dedicated to you; how can we make it better? Any topics that are submitted will be acknowledged, and any topics that make it into a future edition will be credited. Please submit any feedback, ideas, suggestions, or thoughts to Success@ HSGOM.com.

In closing, I'd like to thank you for taking the time to read what is laid out for you on the previous pages. Many people have ideas or goals in the backs of their heads that they plan to put into action someday, when the time is right. This was one of those things for me. Along the way I realized there is never a 'good time' to take on that 'someday' project, because life gets in the way. Don't wait for the perfect time to pursue your dreams. Learn as much as you can about the things that interest you, make a success plan for yourself, and make it happen.

Start today. You can do it!

ABOUT THE AUTHOR

Jim got his big writing break as a junior in High School for the Talisman, the official school newspaper for Appleton West. He wrote a goofball column that in his view was mostly forgettable, until over 20 years later his phone rang one night and the anonymous voice on the other end of the line was reading articles he wrote for the paper 20+years earlier.

Throughout his business career, Jim did a lot of business writing, including a two year stint when he wrote a widely read column called *The High Plains Drifter* for *foodservicerumors.com.*

The idea for *The High School Graduates Owner's Manual* came next. Jim knew a lot about the topic, mistakes that you make when you are young because you don't know any better. Combine that with recognition that there were very few decent graduation gift options for High School Graduates, and *The High School Graduates Owner's Manual* was born.

Jim is very grateful to his family and friends that have supported this project from the start. He looks forward to updating this work every year, and hopefully providing something of value to help our next generation of young adults with a few clues to help them realize their ultimate success much earlier in life.

Jim Egan lives in Neenah, WI with his wife Joan, their dog Bootie Pie and cat Chimpee. Jim and Joan have 2 grown children that they are very proud of. Jay lives in Portland, OR, and Kerry in Madison, WI.

CPSIA information can be obtained
at www.ICGtesting.com
Printed in the USA
LVOW10s0524040617
536869LV00002B/10/P

9 781681 021775